HELEN KELLER

DISCOVER THE LIFE OF AN AMERICAN LEGEND

Don McLeese

Rourke
Publishing LLC
Vero Beach, Florida 32964

www.rourkepublishing.com

PHOTO CREDITS: all photographs courtesy of the American Foundation for the Blind, Helen Keller Archives.

Cover: *Helen Keller as a mature woman*

Editor: Frank Sloan

Cover design by Nicola Stratford

Library of Congress Cataloging-in-Publication Data

McLeese, Don.
  Helen Keller / Don McLeese.
     p. cm. — (Discover the life of an American legend)
Summary: Introduces the life of Helen Keller, who became blind and deaf as the result of a childhood fever but learned to read, speak, and write, and traveled the world as an advocate for people with disabilities.
Includes bibliographical references and index.
  ISBN 1-58952-302-4 (hardcover)
  1. Keller, Helen, 1880-1968—Juvenile literature. 2. Blind-deaf women—United States—Biography—Juvenile literature. [1. Keller, Helen, 1880-1968. 2. Blind. 3. Deaf. 4. People with disabilities. 5. Women—Biography.] I. Title. II. American legends (Vero Beach, Fla.)
  HV1624.K4 M34 2002
  362.4'1'092—dc21

                  2002004097

Printed in the USA

W/W

TABLE OF CONTENTS

BLIND AND DEAF

Helen Keller was **blind** and **deaf**. She couldn't see, and she couldn't hear. When Helen was a girl, people who were blind and deaf were often kept away from the rest of the world. They were sent to live in places called **asylums**.

Helen as a young girl

Helen was very brave and very smart. She learned to speak and to understand words, even though she couldn't hear them. She showed that blind and deaf people could live with the rest of the world. She wrote books and traveled all over. Today, blind and deaf people have a much better life because of Helen Keller.

Helen and a friend with Helen's special typewriter

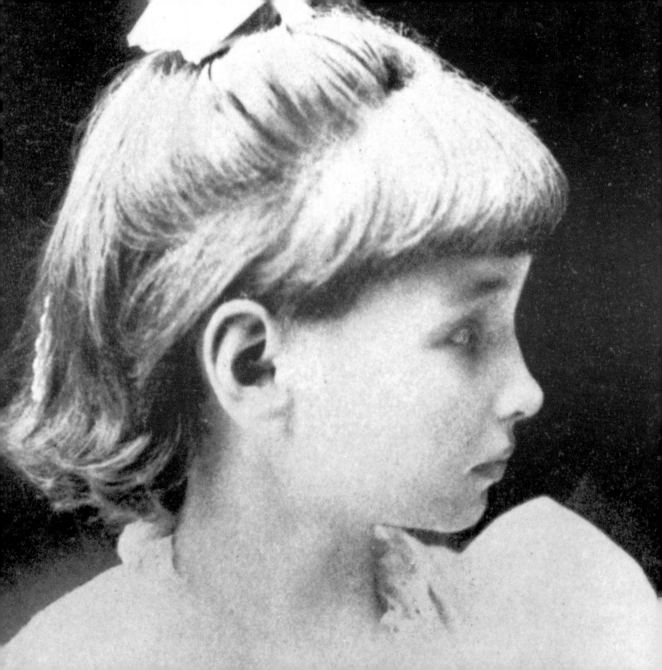

A HEALTHY BABY

Helen was born on June 27, 1880. She lived with her parents in Tuscumbia, Alabama. When she was born, she could see and hear just fine. She couldn't talk, because she wasn't old enough, but her parents talked to her. She was just like any other baby.

A BAD FEVER

When Helen was just a year and a half old, she got a very bad **fever**. In those days, doctors called this sickness "brain fever." They thought it would keep anyone who had it from being smart. When the fever went away, Helen could no longer see or hear.

WILD CHILD

When other girls went to school, Helen couldn't. It made her mad that she couldn't hear what other people were saying. She was called a "wild child," because it was so hard to teach her or make her behave. Other people told Helen's parents to put her in an asylum, but they didn't want to.

A photograph of Helen taken about 1893

13

HER OWN TEACHER

Instead, her parents found a teacher for Helen. Her name was Anne Sullivan. She was only 21 years old. She had once been blind, but an **operation** let her see again. In 1887, Anne came to be with the Kellers. Helen later called this, "The most important day I can remember in my life."

Anne Sullivan

W-A-T-E-R

One day, Anne pumped water on Helen's hand.
Then the teacher traced the letters "w-a-t-e-r" with
her finger on Helen's hand. Suddenly, Helen
understood that these letters meant "water." She
began to learn more words very quickly, including her
own name. She showed that she was very smart.

*Anne taught Helen to spell words
with her finger on Helen's hand.*

CITIZEN OF THE WORLD

Before long, Helen could read, write, and talk as well as people who could see and hear. As an adult, she wrote 14 books and gave many speeches, showing that other blind and deaf people could learn as well as she had. She visited 35 countries. She called herself "a **citizen** of the world."

Helen traveled a great deal.   19

HER LEGEND LIVES ON

Helen Keller died on June 1, 1968. By then she had become one of the most famous women in the world.

*Anne and Helen received
many honors.*

Helen showed that people who were blind and deaf didn't need to be shut away or give up hope. They could learn and live as well as anyone. Helen Keller was a hero and an **inspiration** to the world.

GLOSSARY

asylums (uh SY lumz) — places for people who can't take care of themselves and live with the rest of society.

blind (BLYND) — unable to see.

citizen (SIT uh zen) — someone who lives in a particular town, city or country

deaf (DEFF) — unable to hear.

fever (FEE vur) — a higher than normal body temperature.

inspiration (INN spur RAY shun) — someone or something to look up to.

INDEX

Further Reading

Dash, Joan. *World at Her Fingertips: The Story of Helen Keller.* Scholastic, Inc., 2000.
Sullivan, George E. *Helen Keller.* Scholastic, Inc., 2001.
Walker, Pamela. *Helen Keller.* Children's Press, 2001.

Websites To Visit

http://www.greatwomen.org/women.php?action:viewone&;id:91
http://www.helenkeller.org/bio/graphicversion.html
http://www.afb.org/info_documents.asp?collectionid:1

About The Author

Don McLeese is an award-winning journalist whose work has appeared in many newspapers and magazines. He is a frequent contributor to the World Book Encyclopedia. He and his wife, Maria, have two daughters and live in West Des Moines, Iowa.

$20.64

DATE